Robert's Rules of Order

A comprehensive guide to Robert's Rules of Order

Table of Contents

Introduction 1

Chapter 1: The History Of Robert's Rules Of Order 3

Chapter 2: What Are Robert's Rules Of Order 7

Chapter 3: The Benefits Of Robert's Rules Of Order 28

Chapter 4: How To Implement Robert's Rules In An Organization 31

Chapter 5: Frequently Asked Questions About Robert's Rules 36

Conclusion 40

Introduction

Firstly, thank you for choosing this book. Secondly, congratulations! You have just taken the first step to managing effective and successful meetings.

Do you feel that your meetings are not as fruitful or organized as you would like them to be? What if I told you there is a straightforward procedure that you can follow that will really help you get the most out of your meetings? It's called Robert's Rules of Order and this book will show you exactly what these rules are and how you can apply them.

Robert's Rules of Order is a book that was first published in 1876 and was designed to bring order and a fair system to managing organizations, assemblies, and committees. It aimed to bring a democratic system to the making of decisions among groups of people and create a structure that allowed everyone to have their voice heard during a decisive meeting. Fast forward to the present day and Robert's Rules of Order has been revised and republished several times to accommodate evolving structures and feedback over the last century. The latest edition – the eleventh one – was published in 2011 and includes all of the previous works plus more modern-day revisions.

My book takes a fresh look at these rules and presents them in an easy to understand way and shows you how you can implement them into your organization, whether you run a sports club or non-profit business. It will improve communication between members or employees and make meetings far more effective. Decisions can be made efficiently and fairly, based on a formal debate that is followed by a regulated vote. There seems to be a lot of rules to get to know in the beginning, but once you start to understand them, you will see how they are mostly just common sense and are actually quite easy to apply to your meetings.

There is lots of information online about Robert's Rules and obviously there are the books themselves. Yet, this information is heavy to read and the facts online are scattered all over the place. This book reconciles this dispersed information into one, accessible source of the main key facts of Robert's Rules and allows you to start using them straight away.

This book will help you structure your meetings more efficiently and get far more meaningful debates and decisions from your organization's members.

So without further ado, let's dive right into the first chapter and see where Robert's Rules all began.

Chapter 1: The History Of Robert's Rules Of Order

In this chapter, we will go back to 1876 and discover where Robert's Rules of Order came from and how they have evolved since then. This will help you understand what origins they came from and how they are useful for meetings in today's world.

Let's begin with a brief introduction to what Robert's Rules of Order are.

To put it into simple terms, Robert's Rules of Order are best practices to manage and organize meetings. However, they are much more than that; they are widely-adopted rules that help streamline meetings and make them more effective.

These rules have become the most popular manual to define the customs, rules, and ethics of gatherings or meetings that are used to make group decisions and debate issues; while at the same time, always aiming to reduce conflict and friction. They are used in many different types of organizations, from non-profit groups, trade unions, and school boards to corporate business, church groups, and various associations.

Before we look in deeper detail at Robert's Rules, let's take a look at its history and see where this methodology came from.

The History Of Robert's Rules

Robert's Rules all began back in 1876 when an engineering officer in the U.S. army called Henry Martyn Robert published a book under the title of Pocket Manual of Rules of Order' for Deliberative Assemblies with the subtitle Robert's Rules of Order.

You may think that the rules have some military connection given that Robert worked in the army - yet they don't. In fact, the rules are vaguely fashioned on the procedures used in the United States House of Representatives, which Robert thought would be useful and applicable into the everyday society, with a little adaptation.

So, why did an engineering officer in the U.S. Army trouble himself to create a book based on parliamentary procedure? The seed was planted in 1863 when Robert was asked to chair a church meeting. He took on the position but the fact he didn't know the correct procedure to lead such a meeting bothered him. This niggling feeling followed him when he later participated in different organizations as a member and he began to realize that there wasn't any consistent procedure on how to properly manage a meeting; everyone had their own thoughts and feelings on the 'correct' way, which often led to chaos. He felt this lack of structure prevented an organization – in any area – to properly complete its work, and he decided that what organizations needed was a book that introduced one clear set of rules that could be widely adopted. And so was born the first edition of Robert's Rules.

Many editions followed. Even before Robert died in 1923, he himself had published a grand total of four editions. Each new edition included revisions that were the result of feedback from hundreds of people, giving the books increasingly more authority as it considered the reality of people and organizations across a wide playing field. The first three editions were all titled Pocket Manual Of Rules of Order for Deliberative Assemblies: Robert's Rules of Order and the fourth edition saw a change to Robert's Rules of Order Revised.

However, Robert's death didn't leave Robert's Rules forever shaped by the advice and experience from the year 1915 (when the fourth edition was published). Under the same title as the fourth edition, two more editions were published by Robert's family, and later by his association that was created by them. In 1970, a seventh edition was published under a new name, Robert's Rules of Order Newly Revised, followed by a further four editions with the same title. The most recent one published, in 2011, includes the content of all the other editions plus additional revisions, making it the most complete of all the books.

So, now we know the origin of Robert's Rules, let's take a look at what their purpose actually is.

The Purpose Of Robert's Rules

The whole idea of Robert's Rules is to guide members of an organization to conduct successful meetings and make effective group decisions. It aims to consider everyone's point of view and reach a consensus in the minimum amount of time under all circumstances, from an environment where everyone readily agrees with each other, to one where everyone's opinions are deeply conflicting.

The book was created for everyday organizations, not legislative decision-making, and defines itself as a book that presents the general parliamentary law. What does this mean exactly? It means that it lays out the everyday rules and customs for doing business and conducting meetings in either assemblies or organizations from whatever area. Despite the word 'law', it has nothing to do with what's legal and what's not; rather it is considered the correct way to go about having meetings. It also helps to answer questions that may come up in regards to parliamentary procedure. Parliamentary procedure is simply the rules, ethics, and customs that organizations and assemblies use to conduct meetings. The book acts as a reference for both organizations and members to the best approach to parliamentary procedure. In other words, it is the metaphorical bible of conducting meetings efficiently.

Chapter Summary

In this chapter, we looked at a brief definition of Robert's Rules and their history. We learnt:

- Robert's Rules are a way of managing meetings and to make them effective, meaningful, and fair. They focus on group decision-making in a democratic way.

- Robert's Rules is the easy way of writing them. They are also known as Robert's Rules of Order which is actually short for Robert's Rules of Order Newly Advised.

- The first edition of Robert's Rules was published in 1876 by an engineering officer for the U.S. army, Henry Martyn Robert. His first book was called, Pocket Manual of Rules of Order for Deliberative Assemblies: Robert's Rules of Order'.

- There have been eleven editions of the book in total with the newest one released in September 2011 which includes all of the writings from the previous books, plus more modern-day takes on the subject.

In the next chapter, we will be looking in closer depth at Robert's Rules of Order and understanding exactly what they are.

En ligne seulement

Vive la fin de semaine!

15 % de rabais*

du vendredi au dimanche

Articles de décoration, de mode et de papeterie, jouets et articles pour bébés à prix courant.

Entrez le code promotionnel

DOUILLET15

au moment de passer

votre commande

indigo.ca

Du vendredi au dimanche.
L'offre prend fin le 29 mars 2020.
Aucun montant d'achat minimum requis. Les livres, les articles électroniques et certains autres articles sont exclus.

* Offre en vigueur du 10 janvier au 29 mars 2020 à indigo.ca à l'achat d'articles admissibles à prix courant. L'offre ne peut servir à faire un don à la Fondation Indigo pour l'amour de la lecture ni à acheter des articles de la Fondation, des livres numériques, des articles électroniques et accessoires connexes, des articles American Girl(MD) (autres que les articles Wellie Wishers(MC)), LEGO(MD), Shinola, Casper, et Benefit Cosmetics, L.O.L. Surprise Amazing Surprise, L.O.L. Surprise Glamper, L.O.L. Surprise Chalet, L.O.L. Surprise OMG, L.O.L. Surprise Winter Disco, 4Moms, BabyBjorn, Babymoov, Babyzen, Beaba, Bentley, Bluesmart Mia, Cybex, Dekor, Egg, Elvie, Guzzie+Guss, Halo Bassinests et Dreamnest, Herschel Supply Co. Ltd., Jellycat, Little Unicorn, Maxi Cosi, Mima, Monte, Mudpie, Nanit, Nuna, Oeuf, Owlet, PlanToys, Quinny, RockerMama, SnuggleMe Organics, Stokke, UPPABaby, Valco Baby, Veer, des Expériences Indigo, des cartes-cadeaux ou des abonnements plum PLUS. L'offre ne s'applique pas aux achats antérieurs et ne peut être jumelée à aucune autre offre.

Online Only

Here's to the weekend!

15% off*

Friday to Sunday

On regular priced home décor, fashion, toy, baby & paper.

Enter Code:

COZY15

at online checkout

indigo.ca

Valid weekends (Friday to Sunday)
Now through March 29, 2020.
No minimum spend. Books, electronics & other exclusions apply.

*Valid January 10, 2020 - March 29, 2020 at indigo.ca on eligible regular priced product(s). Excludes books, eBooks, electronics and related accessories, American Girl® (other than Wellie Wishers™), LEGO®, Shinola, Casper, and Benefit Cosmetics products, L.O.L. Surprise Amazing Surprise, L.O.L. Surprise Glamper, L.O.L. Surprise Chalet, L.O.L. Surprise OMG Dolls, L.O.L. Surprise Winter Disco Products, 4Moms, BabyBjorn, Babymoov, Babyzen, Beaba, Bentley, Bluesmart Mia, Cybex, Dekor, Egg, Elvie, Guzzie+Guss, Halo Bassinests & Dreamnest, Herschel Supply Co. Ltd., Jellycat, Little Unicorn, Maxi Cosi, Mima, Monte, Mudpie, Nanit, Nuna, Oeuf, Owlet, PlanToys, Quinny, RockerMama, SnuggleMe Organics, Stokke, UPPABaby, Valco Baby, Veer, gift cards, plum PLUS memberships, Indigo Experiences, and Love of Reading products/donations. Not valid on previous purchases or in conjunction with other offers.

Chapter 2: What Are Robert's Rules Of Order

In this chapter, we will look at the ins and outs of Robert's Rules of Order and come to grips with the key concepts of this system.

To understand what Robert's Rules of Order are about, we need to start with the term 'parliamentary procedure' as this is the very essence of his rules.

That leads to a very good question – what is parliamentary procedure? Despite its formal-sounding name, the term basically means using a simple set of rules during a meeting to let everyone have their say and help make a group decision without conflict and confusion. Knowing these basic rules can streamline meetings, make them meaningful, and let everyone feel that they contribute in some way. It provides a clear guide on how to conduct meetings in any kind of organization.

Robert's Rules encourage organizations to use parliamentary procedure during meetings to make them effective and to use a fixed order of conduct, so everyone knows what they are doing and what is next.

Parliamentary Procedure: A Fixed Order For Conducting Meetings

Here is an example of an order of business for a meeting that follows a logical parliamentary procedure. By following this order, all members in the meeting have a clear sense of order and know what to expect in each meeting, which helps keep everything far more organized.

1. Call to order. In other words, the beginning of the meeting. It's a way of signaling that the meeting has begun, and it is now

time to stop the chit-chat, put away phones, and focus on the task at hand.

2. The names of all members who are present at the meeting will be read out loud to establish who is present.

3. The minutes of the last meeting will be read aloud to recap over previous discussions, outstanding issues, and resolved cases.

4. The officers' reports will be read out, highlighting the important points.

5. Then the same will be done for the Committee reports.

6. Next, the 'special orders' will be addressed. This is the business or issue that the meeting was called for in the first place. It is the main purpose of the meeting.

7. Any unfinished business will be addressed and talked about.

8. Any new business will be mentioned and discussed.

9. Finally, important announcements will be mentioned.

10. Adjournment, or in other words, the end of the meeting.

This order can be followed in every meeting to give it structure. However, it is flexible enough for some points to be skipped – it may not be necessary, or even could be counter-productive, to go over the Committee reports again for example or to discuss unfinished business. The points that are skipped are up to the Chair of the meeting, who can make a carefully-weighed decision before the meeting about which points to address in the meeting based on whatever purpose it has.

So, that's the parliamentary order. Let's look at how members can express themselves during the meeting following Robert's Rules of Order.

Expression During The Meeting

Under Robert's Rules, there is a specific method that members can use to express themselves during a meeting and this is known as a form of moving motions. Motions are just suggestions or proposals made throughout the meeting. Anyone can make them, and anyone can agree or disagree on whatever motion they want.

Robert's Rules suggest that individual members of a meeting can take four different actions, in regard to motions:

• Call to order – bring order to the group if things get a bit unruly.

• Second motions – agree or support with proposals and suggestions in the group.

• Debate motions – disagree or present an argument against a specific suggestion or proposal.

• Vote on motions – reach a group consensus on a proposed suggestion through a majority vote.

When Robert's Rules talks about motions, it identifies four different types of motions (or suggestions or proposals. They are all the same thing, just simply different wording. Use the word that makes the most sense to you). The four fundamental types of motions are as follows:

Main Motions

A main motion, or proposal, presents new items to the members of the group for everyone to consider and decide upon. They come with two conditions: they can't be made when there are other motions being discussed and they always have to give way to the other three basic motions. So even though main motions are important, they are secondary to the others as new business has to wait until pending or urgent issues are dealt with.

Subsidiary Motions

These motions are ranked as more important than main motions, but less so than privileged motions (which is coming up next). Subsidiary motions are the motions that decide how the members deal with the main motions that are presented in a meeting. So, for example, if someone presents a new idea as a main motion, then the subsidiary motions will decide what to do with this new idea. Robert's Rules identifies seven different types of subsidiary motions which are as follows:

• Postpone indefinitely - This means that main motion won't be considered at that meeting and there will be no vote on the main motion. It is basically killed off and not considered at all.

- Amend - This will change the main motion to whatever action is decided.

- Commit or refer - This means that the main motion presented is sent to the committee, rather than the members of the group, for consideration. This is usually done when the motion requires informal debate or when the motion is causing too much debate and so becomes time-consuming.

- Postpone definitely - This is also known as simply 'postpone' or 'postpone to a certain time' and it means that any consideration of the main motion will be delayed until another time.

- Limit or extend limits of debate - This changes previous limitations on the number or length of debates regarding the main motion. The debate surrounding the main motion can be shortened or lengthened, depending on the circumstances.

- Previous question - This motion closes debate, prohibits any other amendments from happening, and encourages an immediate vote.

- Lay on the table - This will halt any current consideration surrounding the main motion and return focus to discussing more urgent or pressing issues.

Privileged Motions

These motions concern issues of great importance and urgency and their discussion is prioritized above all. There are six privileged motions, according to the latest edition, Robert's Rules of Order Newly Revised, and they are ranked in terms of their importance. These motions are ranked from highest to lowest according to their priority.

• Motion to vacate the chair - This is when a proposal is put forward to undo (or 'vacate' as the name implies) a decision that was formally decided before. This motion is given priority above all others.

• Fix the time to adjourn - This is when a time is set for another meeting that will continue discussing the business in the session that is taking place at that moment. It is only a privileged motion when the issue at hand is pending. Otherwise, it is considered an incidental main motion and doesn't have as high of a ranking.

• Adjourn - Adjourning is considered privileged unless it is qualified, the adjournment time has been set already, or if by adjourning the meeting, it would break up the group. Adjourning is used as a privileged motion when it ends the meeting immediately without any room for discussion about its end.

• Taking a recess, or a break - The main difference between adjournment and recess is that after a break, members come back to the meeting room and pick up exactly from where they were before without any roll calling or recapping over the minutes (which would be very counterproductive, if this were the case!). According to the latest edition of Robert's Rules, recess can't take effect when someone is in the middle of discussing something and when it requires a majority vote.

• Raise a question of privilege - This allows a request from the members regarding their rights or privileges as members of the meeting and can be questions regarding safety and comfort, for example. If during the meeting the air conditioning is on full blast and some of the members are uncomfortably cold, a question of privilege could be to reduce the air conditioning level to create a warmer environment.

• Call for orders - This is a requirement that the assembly follows its agenda of that particular day.

Incidental Motions

Incidental motions allow for questions to be asked about other motions as and when they come up. They must be addressed and allowed for before any other motion. We saw above that privileged motions exist in order of importance, yet this is not the case for incidental motions. They simply become the most important motion when they arise and take priority over any other pending issue.

Incidental motions exist depending on particular times and specific conditions. For example, if a member wishes to object the consideration of a certain issue, then this obviously can only happen before there has been any discussion regarding the question and not after.

In Robert's Rules, there are several examples of incidental motions, including: motions that relate to voting and polling methods, appealing the Chair's decision, objection to a question being considered, suspension of rules and a request to read papers or documents relating to the issue. Most of the time, incidental motions are considered undebatable (so when an incidental motion is requested, there isn't a debate about it. It is usually dealt with on the spot).

As you can see, these four motions cover the basic actions that take place during a meeting and help to give them structure. By recognizing actions as 'motions' it helps members understand how they are supposed to act and when, keeping the meeting orderly and effective.

However, it's great knowing that these motions exist, but what we need to know now is how members can present these motions or proposals that follow the parliamentary procedure of Robert's Rules.

Presenting Motions In A Meeting

There is a specific set of rules to present your motion during a meeting that follow a certain sequence. When you want to make a motion, you must follow the order below, which is as follows:

• Obtain the Floor

In other words, this means getting your time in the spotlight during the meeting. To do this, you need to wait until the speaker that is currently talking has finished (remaining courteous and polite is one of the most important rules of Robert's Rules). Once they have finished, rise from your seat and address the Chairman in a polite way by saying, "Mr Chairman". Some assemblies prefer the title 'Mr President'. Make sure you know which one is better before you begin. Once you have said that, wait until you have the Chair's attention.

• Present Your Motion

Now is your moment to make your motion. Speak in a clear way, making your point as concise as possible (all part of making the meeting meaningful, an important part of Robert's Rules). Make your motion positive by using affirmative words rather than saying what you think the group should not do. An important rule to follow is to stay objective and professional – don't let personalities or personal issues sneak in.

• Seconding Your Motion

You've made your motion. Now you have to wait for someone to second (or in other words, support) it. Here, either another member of the meeting will second your motion, or the Chair will. If no one seconds your motion, then it ends there, and the meeting continues as if your motion never existed. However, if there is someone that seconds it, you can move on to the next step.

• Chairman States Your Motion

The Chairman will put your motion before the group where it will be considered and then the group decides which action to take. Two things will happen at this stage. Either the members debate your motion, or they go ahead straight into a vote to make a decision through majority vote. It's important to note: once your motion is in the hands of all the members, the motion is no longer yours and has become property of the group. This means you can't go back and change your mind without the consent of all the group members.

• Expand Your Motion

Now is the time for you to present your motion by talking of its good points and why you feel this motion is necessary. It is at this point you expand on the motion and not when you present it to the Chair. When the motion has reached this stage, you are allowed to speak first, and you must elaborate your motion within the time limit that has been previously set (this is usually ten minutes, but this can be amended at the beginning of the meeting). Once you are finished, you can only speak again when the Chair asks you, or when any other speaker has finished talking. The debate will be directed at the Chair and not the group. This helps keep things orderly and prevents a discussion from turning into a disorganized debate.

• Putting the Motion to the Members

At this final stage, the motion is decided upon. The Chair will check to see if all the members are willing and ready to vote on the subject matter. If so, there will be a vote and the result of the vote will be the action taken.

This is the general procedure that is followed to put forward a motion. The aim is to allow the group to decide on each motion, so all members have power rather than a specific individual. One way to do this is by voting for motions that are seconded to let the group decide what action should be taken regarding the suggestion. Robert's Rules suggest five different methods of voting that are used by the majority of organizations. Which one a particular organization would use depends on its policy, the situation, and sometimes, just preference. These five methods are:

• By voice. This is when the Chair asks the members to agree out loud if they are in favor of the motion (literally, 'all those in favor, say 'aye'). Then, a count is taken, and the majority will win the vote.

• By roll call. This method is easier than the 'by voice' method as it's much easier to keep count. Each member's name is read out loud and when the member hears his or her name, they say 'yes' or 'no' to whether they agree to the motion or not. This is a very useful method when it is required or desired that the opinion of every person in the meeting is recorded.

• By general consent. This method is used when it is assumed that there will be no objection to the motion. The members agree to go forward with a motion by remaining silent when the Chair says to the group the motion will be put in place if there is no objection. There will be a pause when those members that may not agree have a chance to voice their disagreement. If this happens, there will be a vote on the matter.

• By division. Very similar to the 'by voice' method; only this time, members simply stand or raise a hand to show their support of a motion or remained seated or keep their hands down to object a motion.

• By ballot. The obvious advantage of using ballot is that individuals' votes are kept a secret which may be preferable in some cases, especially when the vote is about a sensitive or awkward issue. Voting by ballot involves individuals writing their vote on a piece of paper and then the result is collected later.

Until now, we have seen the parliamentary procedure of Robert's Rules. To recap, this is the sequence of activities that a meeting should follow, the different types of motions (proposals or suggestions), how members should present a motion, and how members can vote effectively for or against a motion that is brought to the table. In order for this parliamentary procedure to work, it's essential to follow the order presented as much as possible, give members time to state their point of view without interruptions and let others respond in a fair and orderly way without any interruptions, encourage members to speak clearly and not diverge (this skill comes easier to some than others and may require the Chair to give gentle prompts if the speaking member goes off topic), and insist that everyone abides by the rules to ensure a fair and straightforward structure for the meeting.

After learning about the parliamentary procedure – or what can be considered the structure, or skeleton, of the meeting – let's look at the common rules for all meetings that will keep the debate fair. The idea of this set of rules is to ensure that all the members are on equal ground and all have an equal chance to voice their point of view in a safe environment, should they wish to. At the core of Robert's Rules for fair meetings is that all the business and issues presented are decided by group consensus – in other words, the deliberate majority decide. It is also essential to remember that the minority have the right for the majority to have made their judgment based on a fair and thorough discussion of the matters at hand. It is then fundamental that all issues are presented in a concise way, constructively debated over, and then decided upon in a democratic manner. The whole point of this is to help organizations and assemblies to avoid clashes and conflicts.

However perfectly the parliamentary procedures are put in place, they still require the members of the assembly to follow them and actively apply them. It is generally considered under Robert's Rules that silence is the equivalent of consent, so if a member wants to object to something, they must speak up!

Points For Members To Consider

Here are some general points to remember for a just and organized meeting. It relates to how members of the assembly should behave when it comes to voicing their views and allowing others to do the same.

• Members should be respectful towards each other, especially when someone else is talking. For a member to have the right to speak (which is otherwise known as 'obtaining the floor'), the member must wait until the other person has finished speaking, and then stand. If someone stands before them, that person speaks. If the member stands while the other person is speaking, this is deemed as offensive behavior and that person will not be given the right to speak, even after the other person has finished talking. Repeatedly standing when another person is talking or trying to interrupt them may result in that member being asked to leave. A person can only speak when the Chair recognizes them and gives them to signal to talk.

• Although, naturally, some members will be keen to start debating immediately, especially if it's a topic they feel particularly passionate about, but a debate will never begin before the Chair has given the signal. The signal is usually a statement that presents the motion at hand and asks if anyone has anything to say about it. This will lead to a sequence of discussions where everyone that wishes to speak gets a fair turn.

- Before a motion is presented to the group, the member that suggested the motion in the first place still has time to make modifications to the motion. If they do make a change, the person who seconded the motion can withdraw their second if they don't like the new motion.

- It is the Chair that signals the 'immediately pending question' which brings an end to the debate and moves the process along to the next stage, which is an immediate vote.

- Sometimes when we feel we have a strong point to make, we want to say it twice; however, under Robert's Rules, a member can have their say once but can't speak again about the same matter until everyone else who wants to speak has had their say. This stops one voice and one point of view dominating the meeting.

- When members express their point of view or wish to make a comment, they must address these to the Chair and not to the person they are agreeing or disagreeing with. Sometimes when tensions are running high about a certain subject, it is easy to let emotions get the best of us, but it is essential that members remain polite and kind (no name-calling!) at all times.

To finish, let's look at the cement of all these points, the glue that holds everything together – the rules and concepts that must be abided by and known of, to make sure that the structure is followed, that members behave well, and that motions are correctly expressed and considered relating to their value.

The Key Rules And Concepts Of Robert's Rules

• Using the privilege motion. This motion allows members to interrupt the meeting if there is an issue relating to basic rights, personal comfort, a noisy environment, and similar matters. This has to be respected and members should only use this if necessary, such as if a lot of background noise means it is hard to hear the speakers or if the room is too hot. It shouldn't be used if a member wants to disagree with something that another member is saying.

• Parliamentary Inquiry. This is when a member is uncertain about a set of rules or perhaps doesn't understand the procedure given a specific situation so they ask the Chair a parliamentary inquiry. The Chair can then guide the member by providing them the information required so that the member knows how to take the most suitable course of action.

• Point of information. This is when another member makes a question to the speaker (usually of an opposing point of view) while they are speaking. Members can do this at any time during the speech except when it's protected time which is the first and last minute of the speech. How does a member interrupt the speaker? If a member has a specific question or statement related to what the speaker is saying, the member may stand up and say, 'point of information' or 'on this point' and nothing more. They are not allowed to specify what they want to talk about at that moment. The speaker can then choose to let the other member speak or can simply reject the request by saying 'no' or signaling 'no' with a hand wave. If they say no, the other member must sit down and let the other speaker continue. If the speaker allows the other member to speak, they have 15 seconds to formulate their statement or question before the time goes back to the original speaker.

- Orders of the day. This is sometimes known as 'orders of the agenda' and is a call from the Chair or from a member to bring the meeting back on track and adhere to whatever the agenda is on that day.

- Point of order. This is when someone draws attention to the fact that rules were broken during the meeting. This must happen immediately when the error or rule-breaking occurred. If there has been a genuine breach of rules, this warrants a member of the group to interrupt the speaker and state why the rule was broken. This then must be sorted out before the issue at hand continues. It is up to the Chair to decide what happens and if it is a case of rule-breaking. If the Chair decides it is a breach of the rules but the speaker doesn't agree, they can appeal to the assembly which will then require a majority vote to overturn the Chair's decision.

- Main motion. As we discussed when we looked at motions, the main motion is a new idea, new business item, or simply the next point on the agenda list that is presented to the assembly. It is the new topics of discussion for the meeting.

- Dividing the motion. This is when a motion is divided into two (or more sometimes) motions that can be acted upon separately. Each part needs to be able to stand on its own, as a total motion, without the need for the other part or parts. A member can request that separate parts are considered at any time, so long as it is before the total motion (before it's been divided) is voted on.

- Consider by paragraph. This is also sometimes known as 'consider by seriatim'. Under Robert's Rules in parliamentary procedure, this technique is used to consider and debate each section or paragraph of a report, a document or an especially long motion. It allows each part to considered thoroughly, in a methodical order, so that all parts get properly agreed on by the members. Only after all paragraphs have been discussed can the entire report or paper be considered as a whole.

• Amend. This includes making amendment to a paper by altering words or replacing entire paragraphs. Any decisions or amendments must be agreed upon by majority vote using any of the five methods discussed above.

• Withdraw or modify a motion. This means that a motion can be taken back or be modified by the member who originally suggested it, but only if it hasn't yet gone to the assembly for consideration.

• Refer to the Committee. According to Robert's Rules, when a motion needs to be discussed at greater length or when it needs a more informal discussion (i.e. free from parliamentary procedures and restrictions on who talks when), then a motion can be referred to the committee. This is known as the motion to commit, and is useful when a motion is particularly tricky or time-consuming. Before a motion is committed, there are a couple of things to consider first. You need to know which committee you want to refer the motion to and include the committee's name when you make your motion (or proposal). For example, you or a member of the group can say, "I move to refer the motion to a committee of eight to be selected by the Chair". This basically means that you feel the issue that you are discussing is best discussed by a committee. In this case, there is no committee, so you suggest that the Chair selects eight people to be a temporary committee to resolve the matter. The number of people is variable; it depends on the difficulty or size of the motion. Once the name of the committee has been stated, you want to make it clear what you actually want the committee to do by giving clear instructions, such as 'the committee is to consider and suggest the best place to hold the annual charity ball' or whatever the request is. You can even suggest a deadline too. These extra pieces of information are important so that the Chair can decide as to whether this motion can go forward.

• Extend or limit debate. This is a particularly useful motion given one of Robert's Rules during a debate: a member may speak twice during a debate on a certain motion and each speech may be up to ten minutes. This gives each speaker 20 minutes of potential talking time which adds up if there are several members in the group and if the topic is one that everyone has a say about. To avoid spending hours in a meeting, you can use the extend or limit debate motion which is a type of subsidiary motion. This allows the group to modify the clause in Robert's Rules that allows up to 20 minutes per speaker per motion to by extending it if the motion requires especially thorough debate, or by limiting it when the need to discuss it at length is not necessary. In addition to extending or limiting the number of minutes each speaker can talk for, this motion can also be used to set the number of times a member of the group can speak, to set the total number of speeches both for in favor and against the main motion (for example, you could propose that there is a limit of three speakers that speak in favor of the motion and three speakers that speak against the motion), and to set the overall amount of time that is allocated to discuss the topic (so you can request a limit of 20 minutes for the overall discussion, for example).

• Postpone to a certain time. As the name suggests, this motion is used to postpone the action of a pending question and reset for a different day or time. When the new day arrives, the meeting carries on from where it stopped. Robert's Rules state that action or discussion on a pending question can be postponed for a different time or day. This may be necessary when, for example, a decision is better made after a specific event has occurred, such as when a certain report has been released, or a survey has been carried out. Postponing a motion can only happen when there is a meeting on the day that the motion is postponed to, and when the postponement date is not too late for the main motion to be effective. For example, if the motion is about deciding the venue for a trade fair that will happen on the 2nd of February, the motion cannot be postponed for the 5th of February as the trade fair is obviously before then.

• Object to consideration. This motion attempts to stop the original main motion from going before the assembly for discussion and must be made before the motion is handed to the assembly. Robert's Rules state that this motion can't be debated and needs a vote to be considered. It will only be enforced if two-thirds of the group vote against its consideration.

• Lay on the table. This motion temporarily pauses the consideration of a pending motion. It is useful when a pending motion is deemed less important than something else that requires immediate attention. Using the 'lay on the table' motion, the pending motion can be put to one side for a bit while the group attend to the more pressing issue. The motion simply puts the pending question on the back bench for a bit without specifying exactly when the group will return to it.

• Take from the table. This term refers to going back to the item that was previously laid on the table and picking up the consideration from where it was left. This can happen either during the same meeting or at a different time.

• Reconsider. Reconsidering a motion or question can be used to reconsider an issue that has already been decided upon, even if it has already been voted on. However, this motion can't be used to drag up old motions from weeks or years ago. It must be within a limited time slot which relates to when the original motion was decided. This is usually on the same day or the next day in the case of a multi-day session or event. Once a motion to reconsider is underway, the result from the original vote will be temporarily paused until the reconsideration is over. The call for motion to reconsider can only be made by a member who voted in the majority vote, so if the member voted 'yes' and the motion was accepted, this member can call for motion to reconsider. If they voted 'no' and the motion passed, then they can't request a motion to reconsider.

• Postpone indefinitely. This motion, in parliamentary procedure, is just another way of saying to kill a main motion. There is really no 'postpone' about it. According to Robert's Rules, if this motion is adopted, it completely prevents the action of the motion. It is regarded as the lowest-ranking motion in terms of importance, so it can't be made when there are other motions (such as incidental, subsidiary, or privileged motions) pending.

• Previous question. This motion also goes by the name of 'calling for the question', 'close debate', 'calling for a vote', 'vote now', and other terms along the same line. It is used to end a debate on a pending motion with the aim to bring it to an immediate vote. Despite its name, the motion has nothing to do at all with a question previously asked or considered, so it's best to consider this under the name of 'calling for a vote' which makes more sense.

• Informal consideration. This motion allows an issue to be considered informally which means the motion is open to questioning and a free debate. However, while debates may be informal, voting remains formal and decisions require a two-thirds vote to be accepted. After the main motion has been resolved – whether temporarily or permanently – the informal approach stops and the parliamentary procedure returns. This motion is useful when the assembly is small, and so an informal debate is manageable.

• Appeal decision of the Chair. This is a motion that challenges the decision made by the Chair. In keeping with the courteous and orderly approach that Robert's Rules follows, the rules state that no members have the right to openly criticize the Chair's decision unless they make an appeal. If a member wishes to appeal, they must do it at the time of the Chair's decision. Any later and it will be considered too late to appeal.

• Suspend the rules. This motion allows the rules of the assembly to be overlooked; however, the reason must be specified. An example of the use of this motion would be if there was a meeting held to discuss firing a member of staff. Your assembly rules include that the manager must attend all decisive meetings, yet in this case, the manager is particularly close to the member of staff that may be fired so feels he can't attend the meeting in an objective way. As a result, he refuses to go. You can request a suspension of the rules to conduct a decisive meeting without the manager and state the reasons why this is necessary. This has to be decided by vote.

Chapter Summary

In this chapter, we looked in greater detail what Robert's Rules are. We also looked at some of the core concepts of his set of rules.

• Parliamentary procedure – the set of rules that helps structure a meeting, an assembly, or an organization – is an important concept of Robert's Rules.

• There are four types of motions (proposals) and they are: main motions, subsidiary motions, privileged motions, and incidental motions.

• There is a specific format to follow when members of a group want to present certain motions and following this helps to keep the meeting in order.

- There are five different ways of voting, and the way used depends on the organization and what is being voted for.

- There are rules for members to behave in a way that fosters a participative and group-based environment.

In the next chapter, we will look at some of the advantages of using Robert's Rules of Order in your meetings.

Chapter 3: The Benefits Of Robert's Rules Of Order

In this chapter, we will look at some of the benefits that Robert's Rules of Order brings to meetings and how meetings can become more effective and successful by using the rules.

Robert's Rules of Order can seem like a mountain of rules to follow; yet in practice, it is much easier to adopt, and the rules become logical. The big question is though: do we really need all these rules and procedures to have an effective meeting? Isn't it just time-consuming learning rules for something as simple as having an assembly to decide something? When it comes to making group decisions about a subject that everyone will have mixed opinions of, it never is as simple as it seems and having a solid structure in place can reduce the time spent debating about points that aren't constructive and help keep emotions in check. If everyone enters the meeting room knowing what to expect and knowing how much time they possess to make their point, discussions become more concise and the order is kept. Also, by fostering a group consensus, it means decisions are made democratically rather than based on the opinion of a select few.

To sum up, here are some of the benefits of using Robert's Rules:

• To make quick decisions, you could simply let the president have all the power and they alone can make decisions on behalf of the group. However, this leads to a dictatorship stance when it comes to decision-making and all actions will be biased in favor of the one person who is making the decisions. Robert's Rules includes the entire group and encourages everyone's participation so that a fair, democratic decision is made based on careful consideration. Even those who vote in the minority can see how and why the majority vote won, which creates a transparent and honest environment.

• Robert's Rules encourage efficiency. They help to keep the meeting focused on the decision at hand, and they encourage people to prepare for the meeting in advance. The structure of the parliamentary procedure ensures that members stay on topic and don't diverge onto different subjects.

• Robert's Rules encourages written records of meetings which creates a memory of all discussions and can be useful to look back on. Having minutes for each meeting is great for cases where certain members of the assembly couldn't attend a decisive meeting and they don't agree with the decisions made during that meeting. They can look back over the minutes and see how the decision came to be, which can shed some light on the situation.

• Robert's Rules were built on the idea of parliamentary law, a concept that has been around for over 500 years. While the concepts have been tweaked over time, the sets of rules are rooted in an idea that has stood the test of time for centuries and has had some of the greatest contributors in the world help evolve it and make it more effective.

• Robert's Rules may seem complicated, but they really aren't once you start applying them. While in theory it may seem easier to just sit down and have a nice, cozy chit-chat about issues and come to some sort of conclusion on it, the reality is, people have many conflicting views and debating about a proposal can often lead to tension and arguments. The best way of keeping chaos to a minimum is to have debates and discussions that are tightly bound by rules and regulations that help narrow the focus, keep things professional, and minimize the risk of emotions taking control.

Chapter Summary

In this chapter, we looked at some of the key benefits of using Robert's Rules to conduct meetings.

• Robert's Rules promotes a participative and group-based environment in which to have meetings.

• They encourage efficiency.

• They require a written record of all meetings which can be a useful document to have.

• They are based on parliamentary law that has been around for over 500 years.

• They are one of the best ways to manage a meeting and keep it meaningful and reduce tension.

In the next chapter, we will look at how you can implement Robert's Rules of Order into your organization and meetings.

Chapter 4: How To Implement Robert's Rules In An Organization

In this chapter, you will see how easy it is to implement Robert's Rules into your meetings, organizations, or assemblies. You will need to set aside some time to inform members of the structure and key concepts of Robert's Rules, but other than that, it is a relatively easy system to put in place.

Once you fully understand the rules of Robert's Rules of Order, then you are ready to adopt them into your organization. Let's see how you can implement them by using the example and steps below.

Let's imagine you are a member of a tennis club that has regular practice sessions, local competitions, and sometimes national tournaments. There are a lot of players and coaches involved, and there are important decisions to be made regarding the management of the club. You want to bring more order to your meetings that are currently not as effective as they should be. You decide that Robert's Rules would be a good way to conduct the meetings and everyone in the club agrees. So how do you go about implementing them? The first step is to prepare for an organizational meeting that will decide the important points of Robert's Rules.

At this stage, you need to make some important decisions and take actions such as:

• The time and place of the meeting. Make sure all key members of the club know when and where the meeting will be held. It is a good idea to stick to a regular day and time that the club typically has meetings.

• Let everyone know about the meeting. If your club already has regular meetings, then it's enough to simply communicate this new meeting in the same way you always do. You can put a note up on the notice board, send emails to your e-mail list, or communicate the idea on Facebook or other social media sites.

• Selecting a Chair for the meeting. The Chair can be nominated and voted for during the meeting. However, as you don't have a Chair yet, you need to decide who will begin this meeting until a Chair is selected.

• Select someone to take the minutes of the meeting. People can come forward to propose themselves as the minutes-taker and a vote can be made during the meeting to make a final decision.

• You need to think of how to communicate Robert's Rules to the group. Perhaps by printing out the most important points and discussing them during the meeting, or setting aside a session specifically for training on the main rules. Keep an easy to access and brief guide of the main rules which people can look at for reference when they are unsure.

• Select someone to present the purpose of this meeting. Will it be you or someone else?

Use this first meeting to explain the key points of Robert's Rules of Order and explain how this will give structure to future meetings. Once everyone understands the rules, the next meeting that the club holds to decide something can adopt the key points of Robert's Rules to help with more effective decision-making.

Before the meeting, it is a good idea to draw up an agenda. An example of an agenda is listed below. This can be handed out to all members of the club who will participate in the meeting prior to the meeting itself so everyone is prepared and knows what to expect.

Club Meeting (Example)

The Purpose of the Meeting (which issue will be discussed on today's agenda)

Date

Time (6 p.m. to 7 p.m. for example)

<u>Items on the Agenda</u>   <u>Minutes</u>
<u>Allocated for each topic</u>

Call to Order and then review today's agenda   5

Review the last meeting's minutes and approve them   5
Minutes

Go over the officers' reports (if any)   5 Minutes

Board and committee reports   5 Minutes

(This lets the committee and the board update the members about their progress, their news, and anything else they are working on)

Discuss old business   10 Minutes

(Here is the moment when past issues are discussed, and progress is checked)

Consider new business (main motion)   15 Minutes

(This includes any events that are coming up such as tournaments, games, and social gatherings as well as general administrative issues that have popped up and need consideration)

Allocate action and responsibility to items   5 Minutes

(This includes allocating responsibility of certain actions to specific members of the group and setting deadlines and plans of action)

Adjourn Meeting   5 Minutes

(This wraps up the meeting and sets the date, time, and place for the next meeting)

*5 minutes remaining as a buffer in case any points above go over the allocated time.

By creating an agenda like the one above, everyone enters the meeting with a clear idea of what to expect and they know exactly when the points they want to talk about are coming up. It also helps implement Robert's Rules of parliamentary procedure into your meetings. You can save on printing paper for each meeting by sending the above template (filled in with your specific agenda) to everyone's emails so the agenda can be read digitally.

Chapter Summary

In this chapter, we looked at how you can implement Robert's Rules into your own meetings, organizations, or assemblies.

• Start with a meeting that will decide the important points such as who will Chair future meetings and who will take the minutes.

• Make sure an agenda is written up before each meeting (you can use the example from this chapter) and is sent to all key members of the meeting, so everyone knows exactly what to expect.

In the next chapter, we will look at some commonly-asked questions regarding Robert's Rules of Order.

Chapter 5: Frequently Asked Questions About Robert's Rules

In this chapter, we will look at some frequently asked questions about Robert's Rules that may help you if you have some doubts about the procedures.

Robert's Rules can be a little tricky in the beginning, but become second nature once you have the hang of them. However, there are still times when some doubts may arise, so here are some commonly-asked questions about Robert's Rules that can help you when you are unsure.

When Voting, What Is A Majority?

It basically means more than half of the votes, although many organizations opt for at least a two-thirds majority. There are some definitions that are best avoided when talking about majorities, for example, 50% plus one is not helpful. Let's imagine that we have an assembly of nine people who vote for the staff party being at the Ritz hotel. Five people vote in favor and four people against. Here it is clear the majority vote is in favor. However, if you follow the definition 50% plus one, it means that the majority in this case would be considered five and a half people (four and a half is 50% of nine, plus one is five and half) so the vote would be considered invalid. It is better to define it either as more than half or at least two-thirds.

If The Vote Is Done Digitally, Can We Round The Number Up To The Nearest Whole Number?

No. Let's say there is a vote with one hundred and one people. The requirement is a majority of at least two-thirds, which would be 67.33 people voting in the same way. If 67 people vote the same way, this is not at least two thirds – it is under, even if by a small amount. As a result, it can't be considered. It would need one extra person to vote.

Can The Chair Of The Assembly Vote?

Yes, the Chair can. The Chair is just as much a member of the assembly as all the other members there and so, as a result, they can vote too.

Do All Members Have To Vote?

No one can force a member to vote, and if they don't want to, they don't have to. If this happens, this is known as abstaining. However, it is better that all members vote as it fosters active and equal participation and is in the best interests of the organization and all its members.

What Is An Illegal Vote?

When a vote is done using ballot, there is a possibility that it can be illegal. A vote by ballot is illegal when: the writing can't be properly understood, the vote was made by someone that isn't eligible to vote, if someone votes for someone that isn't a member of the organization, and when at least two ballot papers are folded together (although this only counts when the papers have writing on them. If there are two pieces of paper folded together and one is blank, it is not illegal).

What Can I Do If An Extra Person Shows Up At The Meeting And Wants To Talk? Do I Have To Let Them?

No. Only members of the committee or assembly are allowed in the meeting, so if someone shows up and wants to join in, it is within your rights to refuse their entry.

A Motion Was Rejected. Can Members Bring This Motion Back Up For Consideration?

In the same meeting, usually not. The only exception to this is when someone who voted in the majority decides they want to reconsider their vote or if certain situations change the motion. In other meetings, members can bring up the same rejected motion under a term known as renewing the motion.

Is The President Solely Responsible For Appointing Assembly Members?

This all depends on the bylaws of the organizations which are beyond Robert's Rules. If your organization has laws that says the president is responsible for appointing members, then that is what happens. If there is no law in place, then it's down to the assembly to decide committee members and not just the president.

Is There A Procedure To Ensure That Items Are Not Added To The Agenda Throughout The Meeting?

The agenda must be adopted at the very beginning of the meeting. If not, then anyone can add extra points to the agenda by making a call to add more items. That is why it is important to establish this at the start as once the agenda has been adopted, any changes or additional items must be agreed on by the assembly with a two-thirds vote. However, the agenda should always be flexible to include new ideas as the whole point of it is to keep things orderly, not exclude new business or topics of discussion.

I Have An Item I Want To Add On The Agenda. How Do I Do This?

The president is responsible for leading the meeting and not for setting the agenda. This means that anyone can add items onto the agenda so long as they do this at the very beginning of the meeting.

Chapter Summary

In this chapter we looked at some of the most frequently asked questions regarding Robert's Rules of Order.

Conclusion

Thank you again for choosing this book!

By now, you should have a good grasp on what Robert's Rules of Order are all about, and you should feel confident to go ahead and implement them in your meetings. It's a good idea to keep this book close by when you're organizing meetings to help you to quickly double check certain procedures if you are unsure. Highlight the points that stand out for you or which you want to remember, to make it easier to recap on them.

No matter what type of assembly you are a part of – whether it's a sports club, a church group, a small business, or a corporate organization – you will find that Robert's Rules can make a big difference in how efficient your meetings are. It will help give group participants a voice which will, in turn, create a more transparent and pleasant atmosphere to debate and discuss in. And we can all agree that this is a good thing.

Good luck with your future meetings! I hope they are no longer that appointment on your schedule that fills you with dread and instead a reminder on your agenda that makes you feel productive and positive!

CPSIA information can be obtained
at www.ICGtesting.com
Printed in the USA
LVHW031739100220
646431LV00004B/554